MAKE YOUR OWN JEWELRY

Felicity Everett and Carol Garbera

Illustrated by Lily Whitlock and Chris Lyon

Edited by Janet Cook

Designed by Camilla Luff

Photographer **Simon Bottomley**
Stylist **Carol Garbera**
Make-up **Wendy Saad** at **Joy Goodman**

Hair **Carlo Braida** at Schumi
Model **Louise Kelly** at S

Rose brooches and earrings (pages 18-19) designed by **Kerry Snaylam**.

Wi⋯⋯⋯⋯era
and⋯⋯⋯⋯

D1451243

Contents

First published in 1987 by Usborne Publishing Ltd,
20 Garrick Street, London WC2E 9BJ, England.
Copyright © 1987 Usborne Publishing.

Printed in Belgium.   American edition 1987.

About this book

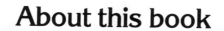

The jewelry in this book is stylish, simple and cheap to make. The book is divided into five sections, each showing a different style of jewelry. You might want to make all the things in one section, or choose a few items from each. Since there is something to suit most tastes, you can make jewelry as presents, or even to sell. You can see the five styles below.

Bright Things

Natural Things

Pretty Things

Classic Things

Crazy Things

Things you need

Clay

Pliers

Yarn

You can see what materials, tools and equipment you need to make the jewelry on pages 30-31 (you may already have some of them). Try to work tidily — it is easy to spoil a piece of jewelry while working on a messy surface.

Instructions

Clear instructions, illustrated step-by-step, explain how to make each item. All the basic skills, such as making papier mâché or clay beads, are clearly labelled, so you can refer back to them if you get stuck.

Design hints

The book shows certain colors and designs for each piece of jewelry, but you can choose your own. Design hints, in colored boxes like this, suggest simple ways of adapting the jewelry.

Choosing what to make

Each section has a patterned border at the top of every page so you can easily see where it starts and ends. Every item of jewelry is coded so you can tell how long it takes and what it costs to make (see the key opposite).

Key

▲	up to 2 hours	● very cheap
▲ ▲	up to 1 day	●● cheap
▲ ▲ ▲	1 to 2 days	●●● quite cheap
▲ ▲ ▲ ▲	2 days or more	●●●● more expensive

Bright things

In this section you will find bold jewelry, painted in bright, abstract patterns. Most of it is made from papier mâché, which takes a few days to dry. But if you are patient, you will be rewarded with stunning results. Below are some of the things you can make.

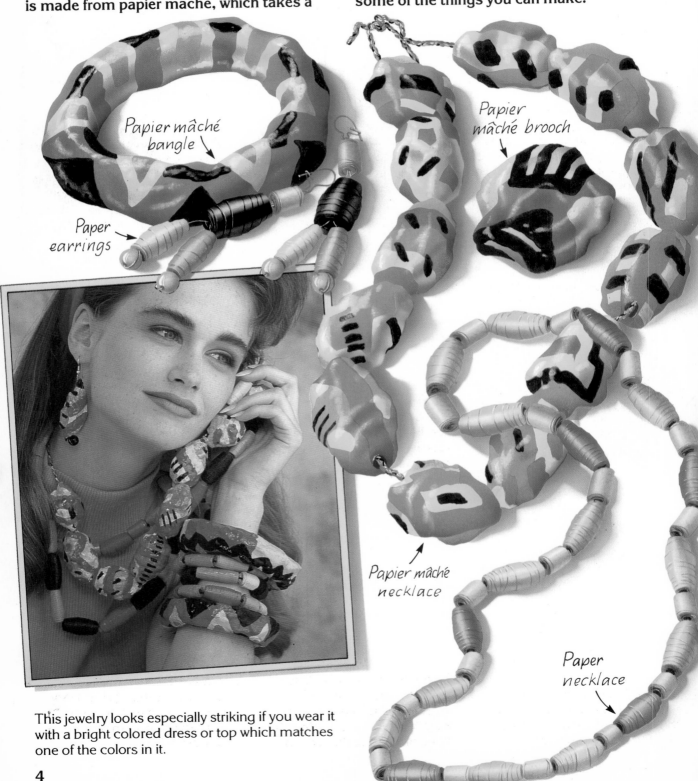

Papier mâché bangle

Papier mâché brooch

Paper earrings

Papier mâché necklace

Paper necklace

This jewelry looks especially striking if you wear it with a bright colored dress or top which matches one of the colors in it.

Making papier mâché

The quantities listed below are for the earrings, necklace, brooch and bangle. Make less if you only want to make one or two items.

For the paste: 1¼ liters (about 2¼ pints) warm water to 250g (8-10oz) plain white flour. In addition you need two or three old newspapers, a dishpan and a spoon.

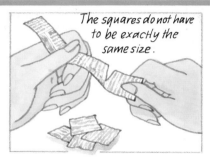

The squares do not have to be exactly the same size.

Tear the newspaper into 2cm (¾in) squares. To make the paste, gradually mix water into the flour in the pan, until there are no lumps.

Then stir in the newspaper and leave it to stand for two or three hours, until the paper goes really soft. The papier mâché is then ready to use.

Papier mâché necklace ▲▲ ▲▲ ●●

You will need:
½ ltr (about ¾ pt) papier mâché
poster paints, fine paint brush and jar
paper varnish and varnish brush
3 or 4 4mm* knitting needles OR
16 to 20 toothpicks
Vaseline
about 1¼ m (1¼ yd) metallic cord and a darning needle
old potato
sandpaper
transparent tape

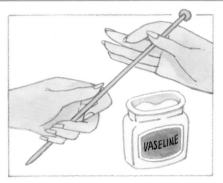

If you want to make chunky beads, cover the knitting needles with a thin coat of Vaseline. For finer beads, do the same with toothpicks.

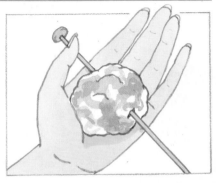

Take enough papier mâché in your hand to make the size of bead you want. Press the knitting needle or toothpick into it, as shown.

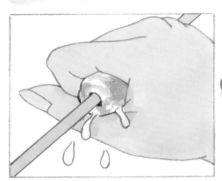

Then mold the papier mâché around the knitting needle, squeezing out the spare paste. Smooth it with your fingers until it is the shape you want.

*English size 8, or US size 5.

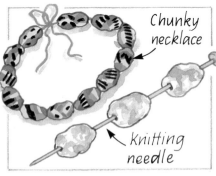

Chunky necklace

knitting needle

To make a chunky necklace, you will need to make 12 papier mâché beads 5cm (2in) long. You should be able to fit three on each knitting needle.

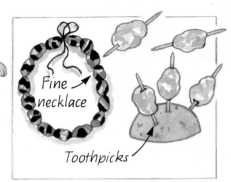

Fine necklace

Toothpicks

To make a finer necklace, make 16-20 beads 4cm (1½in) long. Make each one on a toothpick. You can see how to paint them over the page.

Bright things 2

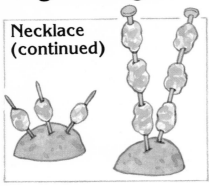

Necklace (continued)

Cut a potato in half and stick the knitting needles or toothpicks into it, as shown. Leave the beads to dry* like this for three to five days.

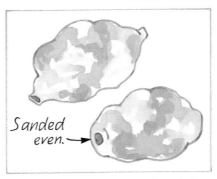

Sanded even. →

When the outsides are dry, slide the beads off the needles and leave them for a day, so that the middles dry. Then sandpaper the ends to improve the shape.

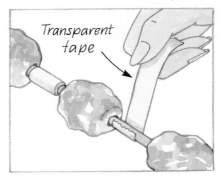

Transparent tape →

Now thread the beads back on to the needles or picks and wind transparent tape around the needle in between each one, to keep them separate.

Below are some ideas for patterns and color combinations.

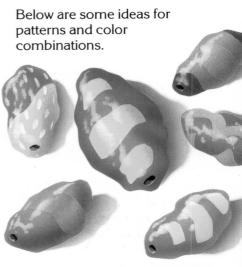

Painting your beads

POSTER PAINT

Paint two coats of white poster paint on each bead. This evens out the surface, making it easier to paint your pattern on later. Leave them to dry.

Keeping your hand as steady as you can, paint a pattern on each bead. Begin with the lightest color you want to use and let one dry before using another.

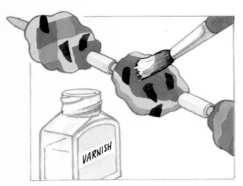

VARNISH

When the paint is dry, keep the beads on the needles, and brush on a thin coat of paper varnish. Let it dry, then brush on a second coat.

Darning needle →

When the varnish is dry, slide the beads off the needles and thread them on to your metallic cord with a darning needle. Tie the ends in a secure bow.

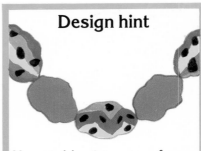

Design hint

You could paint some of your beads with a plain color that matches the patterned ones. Then make a necklace by threading up alternate plain and patterned beads.

*The beads will dry more quickly in summer than in winter. Do not try to dry them over direct heat.

Papier mâché bangle ▲▲▲▲ ●

You will need:

¼ ltr (about ½ pt) of papier mâché
poster paints, fine paint brush
and jar
paper varnish and varnish brush
70cm (about 2ft) 0.8mm (¹⁄₃₂in)
wire (or 30 amp fuse wire*)
an old plate
Vaseline
wire cutters or blunt scissors
sandpaper

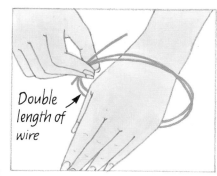

Double length of wire →

Cut** a length of wire long enough to fit twice around the widest part of your hand with a bit to spare. Twist it into a circle to make your bangle base.

Cover an old plate with a thin layer of Vaseline. Using this as your work surface, mold handfuls of papier mâché roughly around the wire base.

When you have covered all the wire, mold the papier mâché into a smooth, even shape. Leave it in a warm place for several days until it feels dry.

Sandpaper the edges smooth. Then paint it as for the beads (you do not need to paint a pattern on the inside). When dry, brush on two coats of varnish.

Two finished bangles.

Papier mâché brooch ▲▲▲▲ ●

You will need:

¼ ltr (about ½ pt) of papier mâché
for two brooches
poster paints, fine paint brush
and jar
paper varnish and varnish brush
an old plate
Vaseline
brooch back
strong glue

Working on a greased plate, shape the papier mâché into a disc with a flat base, about 6cm (2½in) in diameter and 1cm (½in) thick. Leave it to dry.

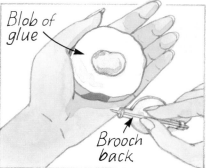

Blob of glue →

Brooch back →

Then paint it as for the beads. Paint the back a plain color. Varnish it when the paint is dry. When the varnish is dry, glue a brooch pin on the back.

---

*You can buy fuse wire from a hardware store. **Use wire cutters or old scissors to cut it with.

Bright things 3

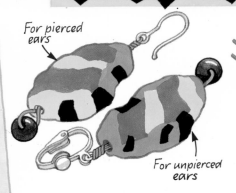

Papier mâché earrings ▲▲▲ ●

You will need:

- 2 big papier mâché beads (see page 5)
- 1 pair clips (with loops for dangly earrings) or ball hooks
- 40cm (about 16in) of 0.6mm (⅟₆₄ in) wire (or 15amp fuse wire)
- 2 wooden beads, 1cm (½in) across
- strong glue
- wire cutters or old scissors

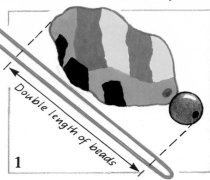

For pierced ears

For unpierced ears

You can make these earrings for either pierced or unpierced ears. Use clip-on attachments for unpierced ears and ear hooks for pierced ears.

Double length of beads

1 First measure your beads. Double this measurement and add 5cm (2in). Use the wire cutters to cut two pieces of wire this long, one for each earring.

Making paper beads*

The quantities below will make three bracelets, two necklaces and a pair of earrings.

Six sheets of colored paper (such as cover paper), 52 × 78cm (20 × 30in), 150ml (¼pt) of wallpaper paste, an old dishpan, a 3¾mm** knitting needle, a thin paste brush, clear paper varnish, Vaseline and a ruler.

Making big, tapered beads

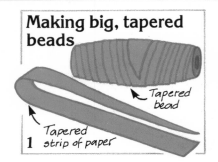

Tapered bead

Tapered strip of paper

1 Cut a strip of paper about 3cm × 78cm (1in × 30in). Then cut it to a point from half-way along, as shown. This makes it taper at each end.

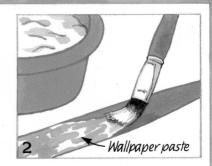

Wallpaper paste

2 Coat a knitting needle with a thin layer of Vaseline. Then thinly brush some of the wallpaper paste over one side of the strip of paper.

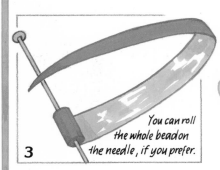

You can roll the whole bead on the needle, if you prefer.

3 Roll the strip around the knitting needle a few times to form a hole, then slip it off and roll by hand. Make all the beads like this.

Making small, straight beads

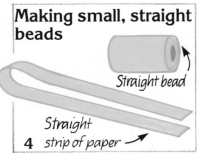

Straight bead

Straight strip of paper

4 Cut straight strips of paper 1½cm × 78 cm (½in × 30in). Then paste them, roll them up and varnish them, as for the big beads.

Varnishing both types of bead

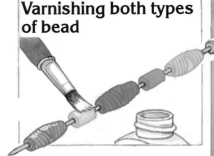

When the paste is dry, put the beads on to the knitting needle, five at a time and varnish them. Let the varnish dry, then varnish another batch.

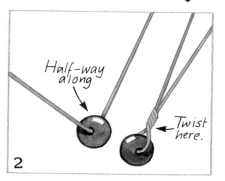

2

Half-way along

Twist here.

Push a small wooden bead to the middle of one of the lengths of wire. Bend both ends around the bead, and twist them together a few times.

3

Thread both ends through.

Thread both ends of wire through your papier mâché bead. Then thread one end through the hole in the ear hook or clip, as shown above.

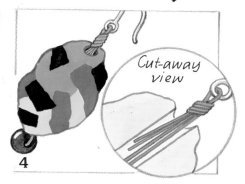

4

Cut-away view

Wind the second end of wire around the first. Then dab a tiny blob of glue on the spare ends of wire and push them back into the earring.

Paper necklace and bracelet ▲▲ ●●

You will need:

For the necklace: 26 big rolled paper beads, **OR** 16 big and 16 small beads
about 1m (1yd) of elastic cord
paper varnish and varnish brush

For the bracelet: about 5 big beads and 3 or 4 small beads
about 25cm (10in) of elastic cord
paper varnish and varnish brush

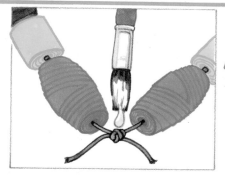

To make a necklace, thread the beads on to the elastic, varying the colors and sizes. Knot the elastic securely, then seal it with a blob of varnish. Trim ends.

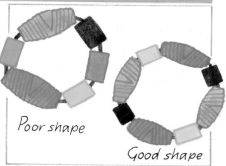

Poor shape

Good shape

You make the bracelet in the same way, but you need to arrange the beads evenly so that you end up with a good circular shape, as shown above.

Paper earrings ▲▲ ●●

You will need:

6 big paper beads and 2 small paper beads
4 wooden beads, 1cm (½in) across
1 pair kidney wires or clips (with loops for dangly earrings)
2 lengths of 0.6mm (1/64in) wire (or 5amp fuse wire) 30cm (12in) long

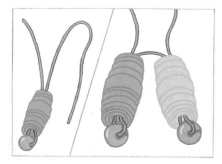

Thread a wooden bead, then a big bead half-way along the wire and thread one end back up the big bead. Thread on two more beads, as shown, doubling the wire through the big bead again.

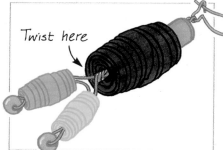

Twist here

Twist the wire at the top of the two big beads, then thread the double wire through a third big bead and a small bead. Thread on a kidney wire and finish as for the papier mâché earrings.

Natural things

The jewelry on the next four pages is all based on primitive shapes and natural, earthy colors. It is made from clay and wooden beads, corks, seeds and leather thongs. Clay beads are quite easy to make. Once you have mastered the basic techniques, you can experiment with different shapes and textures of bead. Combined with plain wooden beads and stained corks, they can look very dramatic.

In this section, you will see how to make the items of jewelry shown here.

Clay and wooden bead bracelet

Sunflower seed earrings

Clay bead and cork necklace

Clay and wooden bead necklace

Ethnic patterned fabrics look especially good with this jewelry.

10

About self-hardening clay

You can buy self-hardening clay from most craft shops. Some makes come in a range of different colors*, others come in just one color and can be painted afterwards. Self-hardening clay is easy to mold and dries to a hard, smooth finish when baked in the oven. Read the instructions on the package before you begin.

Different shapes of bead

Below are the various designs of bead used for the jewelry shown opposite. You can design your own beads if you prefer, making patterns with implements such as clay modelling tools, coins with serrated edges, or pencils.

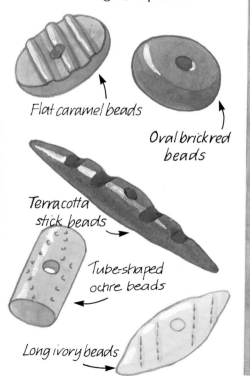

Flat caramel beads

Oval brick red beads

Terracotta stick beads

Tube-shaped ochre beads

Long ivory beads

Making clay beads

You will need seven packages of clay in different colors to make all the jewelry in this section. Choose earthy colors such as terracotta, ivory and ochre, for a natural look.

You will also need a 4mm** knitting needle, an old serrated knife and an old fork, clay varnish, a baking tray and some foil.

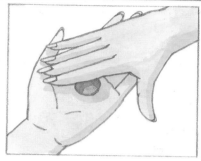

Roll a small piece of clay in your hands until it is soft. Then mold it into a bead. There are some ideas for bead shapes on the left.

The serrated edge makes a good pattern.

Gently pierce the center of the bead with your knitting needle. Before taking it off, mark patterns on it with the knife blade or fork prongs.

For the flat, caramel beads only, carve a pattern first, using the prongs of the fork. Then pierce the center of the bead with the knitting needle.

Check oven temperature given on the package.

Cover a baking tray in foil. Space the beads out on it. Heat the oven to 100-130°C (200-250°F) and bake for 10-20 minutes.

When the beads are cool, varnish them, letting one side dry before doing the other. On page 12 you can see what you can make with the beads.

*E.g. *Fimo*. See addresses on page 31.   **English size 8, and US size 5.

Natural things 2

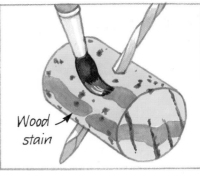

Clay bead and cork necklace

You will need:
1 package of brick red clay
1 package of terracotta clay
½ package of ochre clay
7 new wine bottle corks *
bottle of wood stain
    and fine paint brush
clay varnish and varnish brush
1m (1yd) leather thonging
old serrated knife
old fork
pointed skewer
baking tray and foil

Terracotta stick bead

Ochre tube-shaped bead

Oval brick-red bead.

First make 17 oval brick red beads, 18 terracotta stick beads and 8 tube-shaped ochre beads, following the instructions on the previous page.

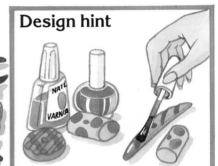

Wood stain

Carefully pierce the corks horizontally with the skewer, as shown. Paint on the wood stain in wavy lines. Leave the corks to dry, then varnish them.

When the varnish is dry, thread the corks and the clay beads on to the thonging. Arrange the corks near the front, to give your necklace a good shape.

Tie a secure knot here.

Check your finished necklace for length. If it is too long, take off some of the beads from each end. Finally, tie the thonging in a secure knot.

Design hint

You could use nail varnish to paint patterns on your beads. You do not need to varnish them again if you decide to do this.

Clay and wooden bead bracelet

You will need:
7 wooden beads about 2cm
    (¾ in) across
½ package of brick red clay
½ package of terracotta clay
about 22cm (9in) of
    elastic cord
clay varnish and varnish brush
baking tray and foil
4mm knitting needle
old serrated knife
old fork

Stretch elastic to seal knot.

Make six oval brick red beads and six terracotta stick beads (turn to page 11 to see how). Thread them on the elastic, knot it, then seal it with varnish.

Some finished bracelets.

*You can buy these from shops selling home-made wine kits and from drugstores.

Sunflower seed earrings ▲ ●

You will need:

100g (4oz) sunflower seeds
1 spool grey button thread
sewing needle
2 new wine corks
1 bottle of wood stain
fine paint brush
1 pair ball hooks or clips (with loops for dangly earrings)
sharp knife
pointed skewer
old towel or rag
varnish and varnish brush

1·5cm (¾in)

Cut a piece of cork, 1½cm (¾in) deep. Pierce it vertically, as shown, then paint on some wood stain. Soak the seeds in water for an hour.*

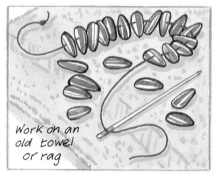

Work on an old towel or rag

Drain the seeds. Then knot one end of a piece of thread. Thread 22 seeds on to it, then thread it through the cork and cut it off 15cm (6in) from the top.

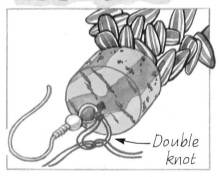

Double knot

Repeat with three more strands, threading them through the same piece of cork. Tie the strands on to the earring wire in a double knot.

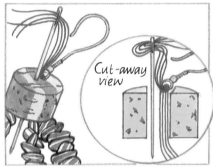

Cut-away view

Thread each end on to a needle and push them into the cork, as shown. Seal the knot above the cork and the knots at the base of each strand with varnish.

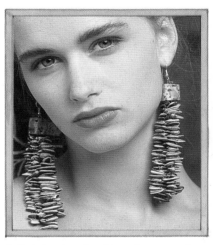

A finished pair of earrings

Clay and wooden bead necklace ▲▲▲ ●●●●

You will need:

1 package ivory clay
1 package caramel clay
½ package ochre clay.
25 wooden beads, about 2cm (¾in) across
1m (1yd) leather thonging
Clay varnish and varnish brush
4mm knitting needle
old serrated knife
old fork
baking tray and foil

Make 13 long ivory beads, 5 flat caramel beads and 5 ochre tube-shaped beads (see page 11). Thread them on to your thonging, starting with six wooden beads**.

Finish off with six wooden beads. Adjust the length of your necklace by taking off some of the wooden beads at each end, if it is too long. Tie the thonging in a knot.

*So that they do not crack when threaded.   **This makes the necklace more comfortable to wear.   **13**

Pretty things

On the next six pages you can find out how to use rolled paper beads, ribbon-type yarn, fabric flowers, marabou and colored clay to make a collection of delicate jewelry in soft pastel shades.

In this section, you will find out how to make the items shown below.

Multi-strand necklace

Rose brooch

Rose brooch

Floral hair comb

Rose earrings

Marabou earrings

Ribbon-covered bangles

Ribbon-covered bangles

You will need:

50g (2oz) ball of ribbon-type yarn* (1 ball of yarn covers at least 3 bangles)
old plastic bangles ½cm (¼in) to 1cm (½in) thick and about 7cm (2¾in) in diameter
strong glue
small elastic band
scissors

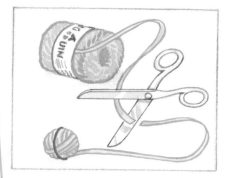

Cut about 3m (3½yd) of yarn off the main ball and wind it into a smaller ball. Unwind 30cm (1ft) of it to start with, and put an elastic band round the rest.

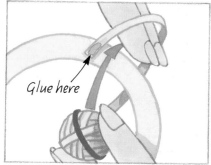

Glue the end of the yarn on to the bangle. Then take the yarn, in a loop, round the outside edge of the bangle and up the middle, as shown above.

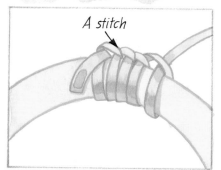

Pass the ball of yarn through the loop and pull it until a stitch forms. Carry on like this, pushing each stitch close to the one before.

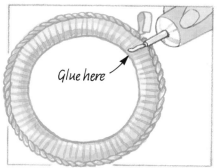

When the whole bangle is completely covered, cut off the spare yarn, leaving a 1cm (½in) end. Glue this firmly to one side of the bangle.

Design hint

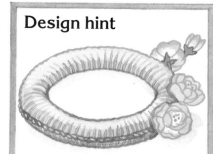

You can adapt the basic design to suit your taste. For example, you could glue a few fabric flowers on to the bangle. Then wind your yarn round to cover the stalks.

Floral hair comb ▲ ● ●

You will need:

about 2m (2yd) ribbon-type yarn
plastic hair comb
strong glue
spray of small silk flowers**
scissors

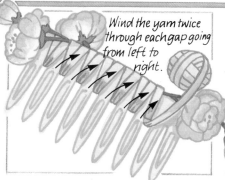

Wind the yarn twice through each gap going from left to right.

Glue flowers along the top, outside edge of the comb. Glue one end of the yarn to the back of the bar and wind it round, to cover the stalks, as shown.

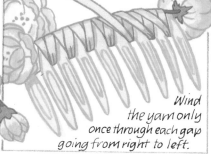

Wind the yarn only once through each gap going from right to left.

Then wind the yarn back to the beginning again, diagonally, as shown, to cover any gaps. Cut off the spare yarn and glue the end to the back of the comb bar.

*Such as *Pingouin Ruban*. **You can buy these from department stores. **15**

Pretty things 2

Multi-strand necklace ▲▲▲ ●●●

You will need:

6 sheets strong white paper, about 30 x 20 cm (12 x 8 in)
¼ liter (about ½ pt) wallpaper paste and fine paste brush
paper varnish and varnish brush
poster paints and fine paint brush
toothpicks and Vaseline
3m (3½ yd) bead thread, sewing needle and screw clasp
88 glass beads ¾ cm (⅝ in) across

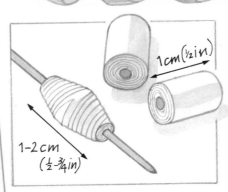

Cut the paper into 87 strips about 1cm (½in) × 30cm (1ft). Roll them into beads (see page 8) using a greased toothpick to form the hole.

Thin some poster paint with an equal amount of water and paint patterns on the rolled beads. Let each color dry before using another. Varnish them when dry*.

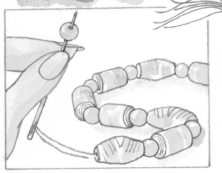

Thread the needle with 1m (40in) of thread. Working on a flat surface, so the beads stay on, thread 31 rolled beads on to it, alternately with 30 glass beads.

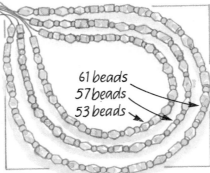

61 beads
57 beads
53 beads

Make two more rows in the same way, using 29 paper beads and 28 glass beads for the middle one and 27 paper beads and 26 glass, for the short one.

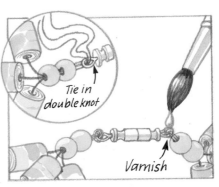

Tie in double knot

Varnish

Thread two glass beads on to all three row ends. Then tie the ends on to one half of the clasp and varnish the knot to make it strong. Repeat at the other end.

Hoop earrings ▲▲ ●

You will need:

pair of silver earhoops 3½ cm (1½ in) across

4 glass beads (or more if you prefer) ¾ cm (⅝ in) across

2 rolled beads (or more if you prefer).

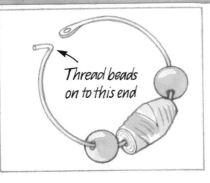

Thread beads on to this end

Paint and varnish the rolled paper beads, as for the necklace. Thread a glass bead, then a rolled bead, then another glass bead on to each earring.

Design hint

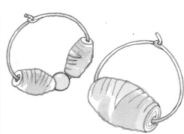

You can use any combination of beads, threaded on to the ear hoops. Try two paper beads and one glass bead, or just one big paper bead.

*They will take about an hour to dry thoroughly.

Marabou bangles ▲ ● ●

You will need :

plastic bangle at least 8cm (3in) in diameter
about 1m (1yd) of marabou*
1 spool of matching thread
sewing needle
about 1m (1yd) ribbon-type yarn (or ribbon ½cm[¼in] wide)
strong glue
scissors

Glue one end of the marabou to the bangle. Bind it with thread, as shown. Wind the marabou evenly around the bangle and secure the other end as before.

Glue one end of your yarn to the bangle and wind it tightly round the join, until it is all used up. Glue the end neatly in place on the inside of the bangle.

Marabou Earrings ▲ ● ●

You will need :

2 wooden curtain rings 6cm (2½ in) across, with eyelets
8m (9yd) ribbon-type yarn (or ribbon ½cm [¼in] wide) cut into 2 equal lengths
40cm (16in) marabou cut into 2 equal lengths
1 spool of matching thread
sewing needle
1 pair of kidney wires
strong glue

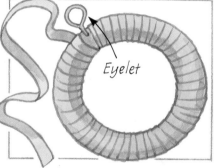

Eyelet

Glue one length of yarn next to the eyelet of one of the curtain rings. Wind the yarn tightly round the ring, as shown. Leave 15cm (6in) free at the end.

Bind together the ends of a piece of marabou with thread. Then glue it on to your curtain ring, so the join aligns with the neck of the eyelet.

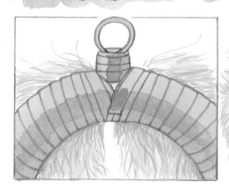

Wind the spare 15cm (6in) of yarn around the neck of the eyelet to cover the join, then around the curtain ring. Glue the end to the back of the ring.

Pull the marabou loop through to the front of the curtain ring and fluff it up. Thread the ring on to your earring wire. Repeat for the other earring.

This jewelry looks good worn with a fluffy jumper.

*Marabou is stork's down. You can buy it from notions departments and department stores.

Pretty things 3

Rose brooches and earrings

You can make these delicate rose brooches and earrings from self-hardening clay.* The ones shown here were made using clay which was already colored, but you can also buy a plain clay and paint and varnish it after baking. Use thinned poster paint and the varnish which the clay manufacturer recommends.

Posy and garland brooches.

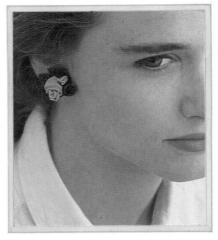

Earrings.

Making the roses

Half a package each of pink, pale peach, green and yellow clay is enough to make all the things shown on these two pages. You could use what is left over to design your own rose jewelry.

The roses are made up from flowers, buds and leaves. They are time-consuming to make but the results are well worth the effort.

Bud

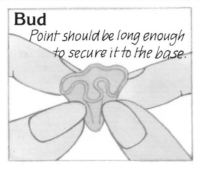

Point should be long enough to secure it to the base.

Make a small ball of peach clay, then flatten it into a disc about 1mm (1/16in) thick. Gently pinch the center into a point.

Leaf

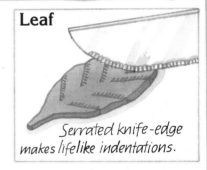

Serrated knife-edge makes lifelike indentations.

Roll out some green clay about 1mm (1/16in) thick. Use your knife to cut out a leaf about 2½cm (1in) long. Mark it with the knife, as shown.

Flower

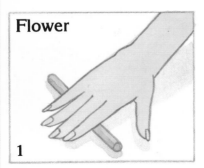

1

Break off a small piece of pink clay and mold it until it is soft. Roll it into a sausage about ½cm (¼in) wide and 12cm (5in) long.

Indentations look like petals when strip is rolled up.

2

Flatten the sausage to make a strip about 1cm (½in) wide. Indent the edges with your fingertip, as above, to make the petals.

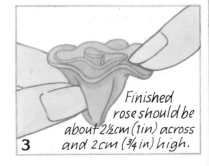

Finished rose should be about 2½cm (1in) across and 2cm (¾in) high.

3

Gently roll up the strip of clay, pinching one edge and opening out the other, to make a rose. Put a dot of yellow clay in the center.

---

*You can find out more about self-hardening clay on page 11.

Clip-on earrings ▲▲▲ ●●●

You will need:

self-hardening clay in pink, pale peach, green and yellow
baking tray and foil
old rolling pin
old serrated knife
clay varnish and varnish brush (optional)
2 clip-on earring backs
strong glue
sharp knife

Make two flowers, two buds and six leaves. Then make two discs, 2mm (⅛in) thick, which will cover your earring clips. Gently press the roses on to them.

Bake the earrings, as it tells you on the package. For a shiny effect, varnish the tips of the petals, when they are cool. Then glue on the earring backs.

Brooches ▲▲▲ ●●●

You will need:

self-hardening clay in pink, pale peach, yellow and green
old rolling pin
old serrated knife
baking tray and foil
clay varnish and varnish brush (optional)
brooch pins
strong glue
sharp knife

Posy brooch

1

Make three flowers, two buds and seven leaves. Make a base about 4cm × 3cm × ½cm (1½in × 1¼in × ¼in). Gently press the roses on to it, as shown.

2

Bake the brooch, as it tells you on the package. When it is cool, varnish the tips of the petals if you want a shiny effect. Then glue on the brooch pin.

Garland brooch

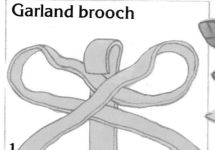

1

Cut a strip of clay ¼cm × 19cm (⅛in × 7½in). Make it into a figure of eight. Cut a strip 4cm (1½in) long and wrap it around the first, to make a bow.

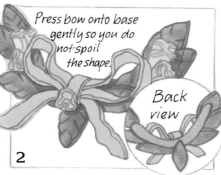

Press bow onto base gently so you do not spoil the shape.

Back view

2

Roll a V-shaped base. Make five buds and eight leaves and press them on to it, with the bow in the middle, as shown. Finish off as for the posy brooch.

Design hint

You can use any arrangement of roses that you wish, and vary the size of the base. The brooch above is made on a long, narrow base.

Classic things

The jewelry in this section is sophisticated and stylish. You can see how, with a coat of paint, old beads and bangles can be transformed into dazzling jewelry. You can also find out how to make glamorous jewelry out of clay and rhinestones and how to make some stunning party earrings from glittery net.

Here are some of the items in this section.

Net earrings

Enamel-painted necklaces

Button clip-on earrings

Enamel-painted bangles

This jewelry looks good worn with a simple crew or polo neck sweater.

Net earrings for pierced ears ▲ ●

You will need:
20cm (8in) glitter-patterned net
1 spool of strong, matching sewing thread
sewing needle
1 pair ball hooks
2 beads about 2cm (3/4 in) across
4 beads about 1cm (1/2 in) across
4 gold washers about 1cm (1/2 in) across
sharp scissors

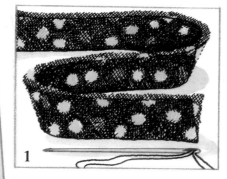

1 Cut the net into two strips 10cm (4in) × the width of the net*. Fold one strip in half lengthwise. Thread your needle with a double length of thread.

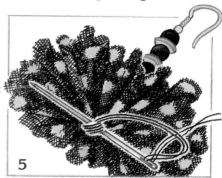

Make the stitches quite small.

2 Starting with a few stitches on top of one another, loosely sew along the fold, through both layers of net. Pull the thread end so the net begins to gather.

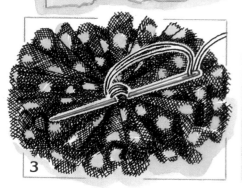

3 Gather the net up until the ends overlap to make a circle. Then sew across the center to close up the hole. Leave 20cm (8in) of spare thread on the needle.

Ball hook

4 On to the spare thread, thread a large bead, then three small beads alternately with two washers. Finally, thread on your ball hook.

5 Now thread the needle back through each bead and washer to the under-side of the net and oversew to fasten off. Make a second earring in the same way.

Net clip-on earrings ▲ ●

You will need:
20cm (8in) glitter-patterned net
1 spool strong, matching sewing thread
sewing needle
sharp scissors
2 clip-on earring backs
strong glue

Make two net circles, as above. Fasten off neatly on one side of each circle. Then firmly glue an earring clip in the center of each one to cover the stitching.

Design hint

You could make either type of earring from plain net, and then decorate them, by glueing or sewing on sequins or tiny beads.

*If your net is very stiff, you may need to use less than the full width of the fabric.

Classic things 2

Enamel-painted necklace ▲▲▲ ●●●●

You will need:
37 beads about 2cm (¾ in) across and 38 flat beads* about 1cm (½ in) across
3m (3½ yd) strong bead thread and darning needle
2 pots contrasting enamel paint, fine paint brush, turpentine, jar, and old newspapers clear varnish and varnish brush
2 pairs 2¼ mm knitting needles**
transparent tape and a potato.

Stick knitting needles into potato halves while the beads dry

Thread the large beads on to knitting needles. Wind the tape in between. Holding each knitting needle over newspaper, paint the beads all over.

When this coat of paint is dry (after about six hours), paint patterns on the beads in the contrasting colored enamel. Leave to dry as before.

On to a double length of knotted thread, thread a flat bead, then a round one, then another flat one. Continue until all the beads are used up.

Varnish here

Tie the ends of the thread together in several double knots and cut off any left-over thread. Seal the knots with a blob of varnish.

Design hint

This necklace looks good in any colors. You could paint an old bangle to match it and make some earrings (see below) for a matching set.

Button clip-on earrings ▲▲▲ ●●

You will need:
2 round buttons about 2½ cm (1in) across, with metal shanks
pliers
2 pots contrasting enamel paint, fine paint brush, turpentine, jar, and old newspapers
1 pair clip-on earring backs
strong glue

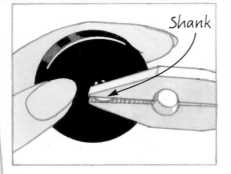

Shank

Twist the shank of the button with the pliers until it breaks off. Repeat with the other button. Working on newspaper, paint both buttons all over.

Earring back

Leave the buttons to dry for six hours. Then paint patterns on the front of the buttons, in a contasting paint color. When dry, glue on the earring backs.

*You could use small buttons instead.   **English size 13, US size 0.

Speckled necklace

▲▲▲▲
●●●

You will need:
300 beads about 1cm (½ in) across
2 pots contrasting enamel paint,
  fine paint brush, turpentine,
  jar and old newspapers
stiff bristled paste brush
2 x 4 row end bars
3m (3½ yd) strong bead thread,
  1 spool of ordinary sewing thread
  and sewing needle
pliers and scissors
strong glue
jump ring and bolt ring

Before you start

The jewelry on this page is patterned by splattering it with white paint. This is fun to do, but can be rather messy so it is best to do it out of doors, on a fine day, or in a garage or workroom. You should put down lots of old newspaper first.

You might have to re-touch patchy areas later

Thread the beads loosely on ordinary thread*. Then paint them on one side with your base color. When dry, turn them over and paint the other side.

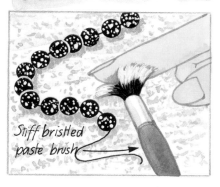

Stiff bristled paste brush

Mix some contrasting paint with an equal amount of turpentine in a jar. Splatter your beads with it, as shown. Leave them to dry. Turn them over and repeat.

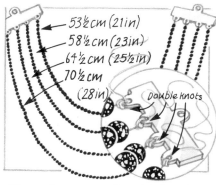

53½ cm (21 in)
58½ cm (23 in)
64½ cm (25½ in)
70½ cm (28 in)

Double knots

Thread your needle with bead thread and make up four rows of beads the above lengths. Tie the ends to the loops of the end bars, as shown.

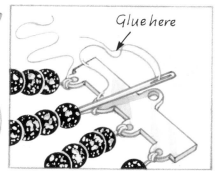

Glue here

Rethread the needle. Run glue along the thread and push it back through a few beads to secure it. Repeat for each strand at either end.

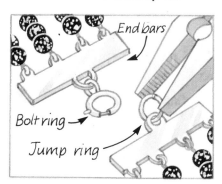

End bars

Bolt ring →

Jump ring →

Using pliers to open and close them, fit a jump ring through the loop on one end bar and a bolt ring through the loop on the other one.

Design hint

You can decorate a bangle to match this necklace, and make some matching button earrings (see left) which can be splattered in the same way.

Speckled jewelry

*If you rest them on a flat surface, they won't fall off as you thread them.

Classic things 3

About rhinestones*

Rhinestones without mounts

Mounts

Rhinestones with mounts

Imitation jewels made of glass or plastic are called rhinestones. Some have metal mounts which you can either clip on to the back of the stone, or use separately for extra decoration.

Rhinestone brooch ▲ ●●●●

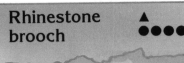

You will need:

about ½ package self-hardening clay (see page 11)
baking tray and foil
tweezers
ruler
sheets of clean, white paper
brooch back
rhinestones for decoration
strong glue

Roll a ball of clay 4cm (1½in) across. Working on clean paper, flatten it into a disc about 6cm (2½in) across and ½cm (¼in) thick, using a ruler**.

Use tweezers to arrange the rhinestones on the brooch, as shown. Then gently press them into the clay with your finger tip, without touching the clay.

Put the brooch on your baking tray and bake it in the oven, following the instructions on the packet of clay. When it is cool, glue on a brooch back.

Design hint

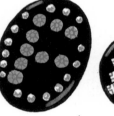

Initial brooch   Small brooch

You can make brooches in practically any shape and size and vary the patterns you make with the rhinestones.

Rhinestone key-ring ▲ ●●●

You will need:

about ¼ package of self-hardening clay
ruler
sheet of clean, white paper to work on
baking tray and foil
rhinestones and mounts
tweezers
key-ring fixture

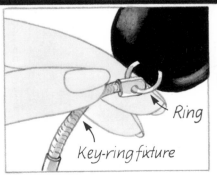

Ring

Key-ring fixture

Roll a ball of clay about 2½cm (1in) across. Push the key-ring fixture firmly into it as shown, so that the ring is half buried in the clay.

Flatten the ball into a disc about 4½cm (1¾in) across. Then decorate it with rhinestones and mounts, and bake it, as for the brooch above.

*See page 31 for addresses of suppliers.   **This is to avoid finger marks in the clay.

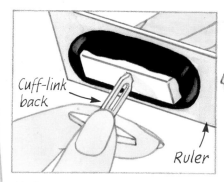

Rhinestone cuff-links ▲ ●●●

You will need:

about ¼ package of self-hardening clay
ruler
sheet of clean, white paper to work on
baking tray and foil
pair of cuff-link backs
rhinestones and mounts
tweezers

Roll a piece of clay the size and shape of your cuff-link back. Flatten it with a ruler on to the cuff-link back, so it extends ¼cm (⅛in) all round.

Make the other cuff-link in the same way. Decorate both of them with rhinestones and rhinestone mounts and bake them, as for the brooch opposite.

Rhinestone rings ▲ ●●●

You will need:

about ½ package self-hardening clay (makes two or three rings)
baking tray and foil
ruler
sheet of white paper to work on
flat ring backs
rhinestones and rhinestone mounts for decoration
strong glue

Designing a round, flat ring

Roll a ball of clay 1½cm (¾in) across. Flatten it with a ruler into a disc about 2cm (1in) across and ½cm (¼in) thick. Decorate it as for the brooch.

Designing a dome-shaped ring

Roll an oval piece of clay about 2cm (1in) long and 1cm (½in) high. Flatten one side of it with a ruler. Decorate it as for the brooch opposite.

Finishing the rings

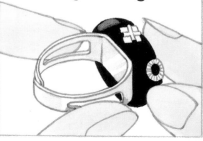

Bake the decorated clay in the oven, following the instructions on the packet. When it is cool, glue the clay on to the ring backs, as shown.

Design hint

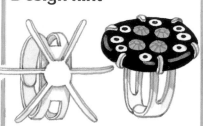

Instead of using a flat ring back, you could mount the round, flat ring on a claw-shaped ring back, so that the tips of the claws stick out round the edge.

Rhinestone jewelry.

Crazy things

The jewelry in this section is bright and fun to wear. You can find out how to make woolly pom poms with left-over yarn, and adapt them to make various kinds of jewelry.

There are also lots of ideas for making crazy jewelry out of children's toys.

Here are some of the things you will find on the next three pages.

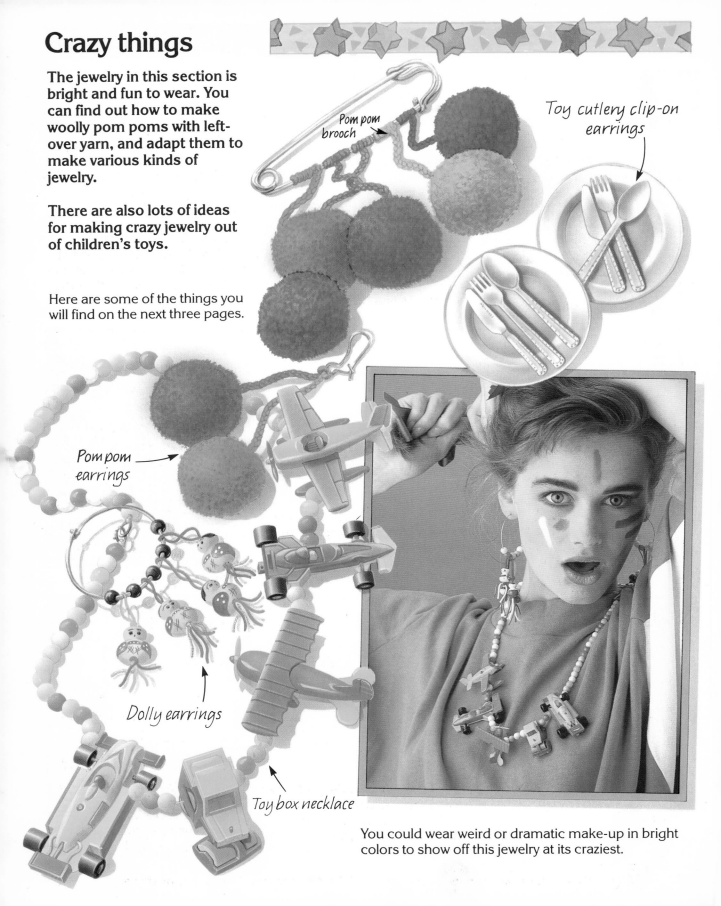

Pom pom brooch

Toy cutlery clip-on earrings

Pom pom earrings

Dolly earrings

Toy box necklace

You could wear weird or dramatic make-up in bright colors to show off this jewelry at its craziest.

Toy box necklace

You will need:

5 plastic toys such as miniature cars, trains and planes, plastic animals, dolls house furniture etc

82 plastic beads about 1cm (½in) across

about 1½m (5ft) strong bead thread

sewing needle

jump ring and bolt ring

scissors

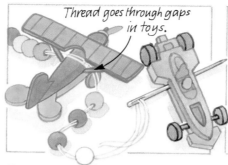

Thread goes through gaps in toys.

Thread your needle with double thread. Leaving 10cm (4in) at the start, thread on 33 beads*. Thread the toys, with about four beads between each one.

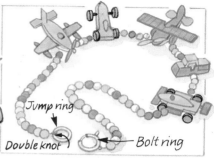

Jump ring

Double knot

Bolt ring

Thread 33 more beads, leaving 10cm (4in) of thread at the end. Tie on a bolt ring at one end and a jump ring at the other and trim off the spare thread.

Cutlery brooch and clip-on earrings

You will need:

3 sets of miniature plastic or metal cutlery and plates **

strong glue

clip-on earring backs

brooch back

scrap paper to work on

Glue cutlery where you like

Glue the cutlery firmly on to the plates. Glue earring clips on to the backs of two plates and a brooch back on to the back of a third and leave them to dry.

Cutlery earrings and brooch.

Dolly earrings

You will need:

1 pair of ear hoops about 3½cm (1½ in) across

8 little wooden dolls (or Christmas decorations) with hanging loops

10 plastic beads about 1cm (½ in) across

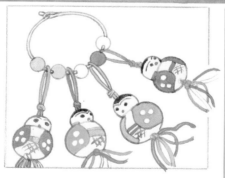

Thread up four wooden dolls (or Christmas decorations) on each ear hoop, alternately with five plastic beads. Start and finish with a bead.

Design hint

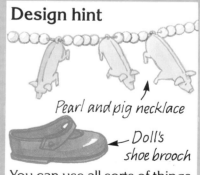

Pearl and pig necklace

Doll's shoe brooch

You can use all sorts of things to design your own crazy jewelry. The basic techniques stay the same. Above are some ideas.

*Work on a flat surface so the beads stay on the thread.   **You can buy these from some toy shops.

Crazy things 2

Making a woolly pom pom and chain

Dotted lines show how to find centre of card square.

Thread yarn on to darning needle when hole gets small.

1

2

You need spare double knitting yarn, a piece of card 7cm (3in) square, a pencil, sharp scissors, a crochet hook and a darning needle.

On double card, draw a 3½cm (1¼in)* diameter circle. Draw a 2cm (¾in) diameter circle in the middle of it. Cut them out to make two rings.

Wind your yarn into a ball which will fit through the center hole. Then tie the end on to the two rings and wind the yarn around them.

Loose slip knot

Leave 5cm (2ins) of yarn here.

3

4

5

When the hole is full, cut the yarn between the rings. Part them and tie a piece of yarn 75cm (30in) long, tightly around the middle.

Tear off the card rings and fluff out the pom pom. Tie a loose slip knot in the yarn ends, as close to the pom pom as you can make it.

Put your crochet hook through the slip knot as shown. Hold the crochet hook and pom pom in your right hand and the yarn, as shown, in your left.

Pull yarn through here.

End loop. Pull to fasten off.

6

7

Holding the slip knot in your left hand, catch a loop of double yarn with the crochet hook and draw it through the loop of your slip knot.

Carry on until the chain is the length you want it. Then hook the yarn through the end loop and pull tight. Leave the ends 18cm (7in) long.

Design hint

You can make a two-tone pom pom. First work a few rounds of one color, then change to another color.

*You can make bigger or smaller pom poms by varying the size of your card rings.

Pom pom earrings ▲▲ ●

You will need:

2 pom poms with chains 5cm (2in) long

2 pom poms with chains 7cm (3in) long

scissors

darning needle

pair of kidney wires

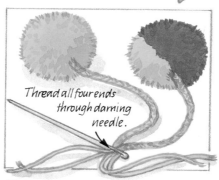

Thread all four ends through darning needle.

Make two pom poms with 5cm (2in) chains and two with 7cm (3in) chains. Thread the yarn ends of one long and one short chain on to a darning needle.

Kidney wire goes through here.

Neatly darn the four yarn ends into the chains, as shown. Thread a kidney wire through the join at the top. Make another earring in the same way.

Pom pom brooch ▲▲ ●

You will need:

5 pom poms with chains about 7cm (3in) long

darning needle

kilt pin (or a giant safety pin) about 6cm (2½in) long

scissors

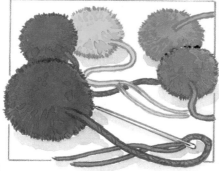

Make five pom poms, each with a chain about 7cm (3in) long. Thread the spare yarn at the ends of one chain on to your darning needle.

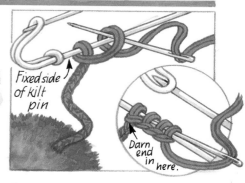

Fixed side of kilt pin

Darn end in here.

Stitch the yarn ends over the fixed side of the kilt pin. Then stitch for another 1cm (½in), as shown. To finish off, darn the ends into the crochet chain.

Repeat with the other four pom poms. When you have stitched them all on, the metal on the fixed side of the kilt pin should be covered with yarn.

Design hint

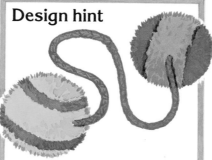

You can turn pom poms into almost anything. For instance you can make a hair bobble by stitching together two big pom poms on long chains.

The finished pom pom jewelry.

*A kilt pin is a giant safety pin. You can buy them from notions departments.

Tools, equipment and materials

Here you can find out about the things you need to make the jewelry. If you have problems finding the more unusual items, you may be able to order them by post. Many companies have a mail order service and there are some useful addresses opposite.

Findings

The metal components needed to make jewelry (known as findings) can be bought from specialist craft shops (see addresses opposite).

For earrings

Pierced ears:

Kidney wire

Metal ear hoop

Ball hook

Unpierced ears:

Clip (with loop for dangly earrings).

Screw (with loop for dangly earrings).

Clip-on earring back.

Screw-on earring back.

For necklaces

Screw clasp with loops.

Bolt ring and jump ring.

Jump ring and hook.

End bar.

For brooches

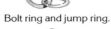
Brooch pin

Brooch back

For key-rings, cuff-links and rings

Cuff link backs   Ring backs   Key ring fixture

Wire (for earrings and bangles)

0.6mm (¹/₆₄in) wire (or 15 amp fuse wire) for earrings.

0.8mm (¹/₃₂in) wire (or 30 amp fuse wire) for papier mâché bangles.

Equipment

Jar		Turpentine	
Old rags		Newspapers	
Baking tray		Foil	
Cardboard box (to keep everything in).		Cardboard	
Old rolling pin		Transparent tape	
Old dishpan		Old spoon	

Tools

Ruler		Tape measure	
Wire cutters or blunt scissors		All purpose scissors	
Sharp knife		Small pliers	
Toothpicks		Knitting needles	
Sewing needles		Darning needle	
Paste brush		Fine paint brushes	
Varnish brush		Tweezers	
Pencil		Crochet hook	
Old serrated knife		Old fork	
Pointed skewer		Sandpaper	

Materials

Self-hardening clay (from art and craft shops).		**Strong paper**, such as coated cartridge, or cover paper (from art shops).		**Clear paper varnish** (from art shops). Alternatively, use clear nail polish.	
Clay varnish (from art shops). Use the type recommended for the brand of clay you use.		**Wooden curtain rings** (from hardware or drapery departments).		**Buttons with shanks** (from notions departments).	
Kilt pins (from notions departments).		**Ribbon-type yarn** (from wool shops). Sold under different brand names.		**Sequins** (from notions departments). These are shiny pieces of decorative plastic.	
Rhinestones (from craft shops and notions departments).		**Marabou**, or stork's down (from notions departments).		**Fabric flowers** (from notions departments). Can be silk or synthetic.	
Children's toys (from toy shops) and novelties from Christmas crackers.		**Old or broken jewelry**		**Plain or glitter-patterned net.** You can buy this from fabric shops.	
Sunflower seeds (from health food stores and pet shops).		**Woodstain** (from hardware stores).		**Strong glue** which is recommended for wood, metal and plastic.	
Poster paint and enamel paint		**Leftover yarn**		**Wine corks** (from shops stocking home wine-making kits).	

Beads (from craft shops, notions departments and shops selling jewelry findings).

Wooden beads

Metal washers

Plastic beads

Glass beads

Thread (from notions departments and shops selling jewelry findings).

Elastic cord

Leather thonging

Strong bead thread (polyester, or nylon)

Thick metallic cord

Useful addresses

Jewelry findings

Creative Beadcraft Ltd,
Unit 26, Chiltern Trading Estate,
Earl Howe Rd, Holmer Green,
High Wycombe,
Buckinghamshire, England.

Hobby Horse Ltd,
15-17 Langton Street, London
SW10 0JL, England.

Beadshop,
43 Neal Street, London
WC2H 9PJ, England.

Rio Grande Albuquerque,
6901 Washington NE,
Albuquerque,
New Mexico 87109, USA.

Watts International
Findings Company Inc.,
6024 South Memorial Drive,
Tulsa, Oklahoma 74145, USA.

John Bead Corporation Ltd,
21 Bertrand Avenue,
Scarborough, Ontario,
M1L 2P3, Canada.

Johnston Silvercraft Ltd,
579 Richmond Street West,
Toronto, Ontario,
M5V 1Y6, Canada.

Supercraft Emporium,
33 Moore Street, Perth, WA
6000, Australia.

Johnson Matthey Ltd,
114 Penrose Road,
Auckland 6, New Zealand.

Jewelcraft,
51 Unley Road, Parkside, 5063,
South Australia.

Fimo clay

Available from branches of
W.H. Smith in the UK.

For details of availability
elsewhere, please contact:

Staedtler (Pacific) Pty. Ltd,
P.O. Box 576, Dee Why, N.S.W.
2099, Australia.

Connelly Bros. Ltd,
7 Falcon Street, P.O. Box 496,
Parnell, Auckland 1, New
Zealand.

Accent Import Export Inc,
460 Summit Road, Walnut
Creek, Ca. 90210, U.S.A.

Dee's Delights Inc,
3150 State Line Road,
Cincinatti, North Bend, Ohio
45052, U.S.A.

Index